I0199763

Kingdom Bound:
Our Journey of Joy

By Jeffrey Jon Richards

Resource Publications
An Imprint of Wipf and Stock Publishers
Eugene, Oregon

RESOURCE PUBLICATIONS
AN IMPRINT OF WIPF AND STOCK PUBLISHERS
199 W 8th Avenue, Suite 3
Eugene OR 97401

http://www.wipfandstock.com

KINGDOM BOUND:
OUR JOURNEY OF JOY

Copyright© 2004 by Jeffrey Jon Richards

ISBN: 978-1-4982-4729-0

To Emily Katherine and Lauren Meredith
— Daughters of Promise

KINGDOM BOUND: OUR JOURNEY OF JOY

Table of Contents

The hardness of God is kinder than the softness of men,
and His compulsion is our liberation.

— *C. S. Lewis*

KINGDOM BOUND: OUR JOURNEY OF JOY

⌐· PREFACE ·¬

As a child, my mother would read to me from the book of Revelation, and the images of what is contained in this last book in the Bible became vivid pictures of the conflict between forces of righteousness and evil. Over the years, I maintained an interest in futurology and though no person has been able or will be able to predict the future, one is able to understand generally God's plan for humanity and the world by studying the Bible.

We live in most uncertain times. I have been to Europe on several occasions in recent years, and people there appear to be as apprehensive about their lives and the future as are Americans. Since the apocalyptic tragic event of 9/11, Americans in particular feel and believe that their lives have been placed on notice — we are uncertain how each day will turn out. We hear much about a sound defense system and measures to take in order to bring security in our homeland. But the fact is, there will never be ultimate security in this life. We must take measures to defend ourselves, and to use solid common sense, but we cannot predict what will happen tomorrow or next week.

This book is an attempt to remind us of the quest for ultimate security. If there is a God and this ultimate One is loving and has a plan for everyone, surely there is a means to determine how to enter into a relationship with God and to live a meaningful life and expect a heavenly future. I invite you to read and consider what is contained in this book. I pray that you find meaning, fulfillment and hope now and in the future.

J. J. Richards
Charlotte, North Carolina
Summer 2004

⌐· INTRODUCTION ·⌐

Many people live in fear of a holocaust — either self-destructive or annihilation from an uncontrollable force. During the past five decades, controversies have revolved around the threat of nuclear warfare and the possibility of the destruction of entire cities and even countries. Environmentalists remind us that the earth cannot sustain much more abuse. We are bombarded persistently with updated statistics concerning the gravity of the AIDS epidemic. Famine and earthquakes are a way of life on many part so the globe. It seems that much of humanity has a reason to live on the brink of despair.

Since 9/11, the world has been put on notice. At any moment in the world destruction and mass murder can occur, and for many it appears that there is nothing that can be done to prevent such terrorist activities. The image of the destruction of New York City's Twin Towers, the relentless smoke, and the facial expressions of many who were attempting to scramble to safety can be replayed in one's mind by those who witnessed the sights either in person, on TV, or on the web.

Over the past several years there have been numerous books and extended discussions about futurology, or what awaits the world during the twenty-first century. Many of those who do not reference religious subjects fear that there eventually will be some type of cataclysmic destruction. The Bible has a great deal to say about future matters; in fact, some scholars of the Bible believe that as much as twenty percent of the Bible was prophetic when written or that much of the Bible is history prewritten. The argument is that the ability to foresee is one of the evidences that the Bible is of divine origin and is unlike any other religious book.

I have attempted to survey one major view of the future, a perspective that is popular today not only in the United States but also worldwide. I have also looked at other views of the end times but devote the majority of the material to one particular perspective. Christians believe that God has a plan for everyone in the future. God, who is perfect love, desires to communicate that plan to humanity; some will listen and not accept the offer of love and final salvation, while others willingly respond to His love and presence and accept the future on His terms.

I pray that what is contained in these pages will encourage you, whether you have studied this issue or not. So much of our thinking and perceptions are controlled by the media, which of course has its own biases. I have been involved for years in historical research, and I know the importance of allowing the original sources to speak for themselves. Of course, there is the issue of interpretation, and on many of the particulars, I am not offering specific conclusions as I would not want to insult the intelligence of the reader.

Attempting to speculate what the future holds is an adventure. I pray that your time invested will be rewarding and exciting.

Part One

⤚· CHAPTER ONE ·⤙

COMING EVENTS:
WHAT LIES AROUND THE CORNER

The Role of Prophecy

The Bible is chock-full of futurology or predictions of the future. Most of this has already been fulfilled in past events, much of it finding fulfillment even before the time of Jesus Christ. However, many believe that there is still much which has been unfulfilled. There is not another book in the world which has been able to predict the future as accurately and with such pin-point precision as the Bible. Jean Dixon and Nostradamus are not even in the same category when it comes to the ability to see what awaits humankind in the future. When the word *prophet* is mentioned today, people may have a variety of images and ideas of just who such a person is. Especially after the events of September 11, 2001, many would now think about an Islamic fundamentalist—wild-eyed, full of vengeance and prophesying against anything western. Yet, others might have images of some kind of eastern mystic; whereas, perhaps others might think of a person who is in need of Prozac, or a person like Jim Jones who would be willing to lead his followers astray and even demand that they die for a cause that makes no logical sense.

The fact is the word *prophet* has a long and honorable history. The English word comes from the Latin, *propheta*, whereas the Greek word is *prophetes*. According to Webster, the idea is "one who utters divinely inspired revelations; the writer of one of the prophetic books of the Old Testament; one gifted with more than ordinary spiritual and moral insight; one who foretells future events."

Meaning of the Word Prophet

There are two basic ideas of the word *prophet* as found in the Old Testament. The first one comes from the Hebrew *nabi*, meaning "one who speaks for God." The words essentially would not be the prophet's own, but he or she would speak forth the words as given to that person from God. The second comes from the Hebrew word, *roeh*, and this too is a fascinating word. *Roeh* was a person who could see into the future and could tell what would happen even hundreds of years from the time in which that person lived.

Biblical scholars tell us that about 25% of the Bible is prophetic; that portion of Scripture, when it was written, predicted an event would occur, and consequently this prophecy mandated that the event would definitely take place. Such events as the Babylonian Captivity which occurred in 587 B.C. were predicted hundreds of years before the events happened. Many believe that the prophets Isaiah and Micah told of the coming of the Messiah, whom Christians claim was none other than Jesus Christ. Many scholars believe that the prophet Daniel under the influence of divine enabling was able to tell of the rise of several empires including Greece and Rome. But he also wrote of an emperor who has not yet taken power—many claim that this is the Anti-Christ of the end days.

Some of the prophets were anything but boring. Elijah, for example, single-handedly opposed over five-hundred prophets of a pagan god called Baal. He even won! Jonah preached such a powerful message in the ancient town of Nineveh that hundreds of thousands came to accept the God of whom he spoke. John the Baptist was a powerful and charismatic figure who had a large following as he preached about the coming Messiah in ancient Israel.

13

Lewis Sperry Chafer (1871-1952, Christian Bible scholar/theologian) wrote that much of biblical prophecy speaks about the coming of a future time of blessing for the nation of Israel. Many would agree with Chafer. Chuck Swindoll and David Jeremiah, two popular radio personalities and authors, also believe and preach this view. For almost two thousand years the country of Israel did not exist. Jewish people were dispersed around the world, in exile and estranged from their own land. Zionism, or the world-wide movement to again establish a homeland, eventually resulted in the nation of Israel in 1948. Throughout the centuries, Jerusalem had been demolished several times and under the control of various nations. Though she is still experiencing divisiveness and turmoil, today Israel is a strong nation with a first-rate defense system. During the Six-Day War in 1967 and also the Gulf War Crisis in 1991, she more than proved her capacity of protecting herself.

Why is prophecy so important to Swindoll and innumerable others? First, they believe that at least one fifth of the Bible at the time written was prophetic. Second, prophecy attests to the divine authority of the Bible; prophecy and its fulfillment verifies the Bible as the Word of God in distinction to mere human opinion. Third, prophetic themes enable one to more fully interpret the Scriptures. Fourth, prophecy gives to the individual a "blessed hope" concerning the future. There has always been the need for hope, but certainly our times today express that need more than ever.

The prophets, this view claims, spoke primarily during a dismal time in Israel's history as she was about to be dispersed. But it was in the midst of this period that the prophets spoke of Israel's imminent glory and the establishment of the coming Messiah's glorious kingdom. Many believe that this Kingdom will be a time when there is righteousness on earth—there will be no crime, unemployment, disease and despair; rather, the time will be filled with God's presence, peace, joy and harmony among all peoples. It is believed that during this time, Jesus Christ will literally rule over earth with Jerusalem as its religious and political center. The Old Testament book of Jeremiah 23:5 speaks of the reign of the King during a time when total justice will be upon earth. There will never be the situation of the wrong person sentenced to prison, racism or any other unjust action—for the first time in human history, evil will be checked. This view also claims that the passages of Ezekiel 37:24 and Hosea 3:4,5 emphasize this will be the rule of God, or what is called a theocracy. Political philosophies have come and gone throughout the centuries. Humans have yet to devise the perfect political order. Communism promised so much but left innumerable lives shattered, and overall has proved to be a dismal failure. But finally the world will have a leader who will rule with perfect equity.

Key Passages

The prophets foretold that the Messiah's reign would be centered in Jerusalem where Israel has been regathered and converted (Jeremiah

33:7-9, Ezekiel 36:16-38, 37:21-25). The prophets Zechariah and Malachi speak of the kingdom's establishment through the reigning power of the returning King (Zechariah 2:10-12; Malachi 3:1-4). However, the kingdom is also seen as a period of great spiritual delightfulness. People will want to do good without being told to do so; there will be no forced righteousness during this thousand year period.

It is believed that the majority of the prophetic Scriptures have been fulfilled, but many are careful to say that there are many events which will yet be played out such as the following: the Rapture of the Church, the Great Tribulation, the coming of the Anti-Christ, more suffering for Israel, the Second Coming of Christ, the Battle of Armageddon, the binding of Satan, the kingdom, the doom of Satan, the Great White Throne Judgment, and finally the new heaven and earth. All of the above events, it is believed, will follow consecutively with the doom of Satan and the Great White Throne Judgment occurring after the thousand years of Messiah's reign. These events are just as certain to occur as those events which are now recorded history.

The Question of the Rapture

An issue which has divided and continues to cause controversy among many is the view of whether or not there will be a rapture, or a taking up, of all Christians before the actual Second Coming of Christ.

Without going into detail, the idea for a catching up of the saints is believed to be grounded in two major Biblical passages — Daniel 9:24-27 and I Thessalonians 4:13-18. The Daniel passages refer to a period of seventy weeks, which many biblical scholars say is a period of 490 years (one week in this case is interpreted to be a period of seven years; therefore, seventy weeks would be equal to a time of 490 years). We find in Daniel 9:24-27, the following:

> Seventy weeks are decreed for your people and your holy city to finish transgression, to put an end to sin, to atone for wickedness, to bring in everlasting righteousness, to seal up vision and prophecy and to anoint the most holy.
>
> Know and understand this: From the issuing of the decree to restore and rebuild Jerusalem until the Anointed One, the ruler, comes, there will be seven "sevens," and sixty-two "sevens." It will be rebuilt with streets and a trench, but in times of trouble. After the sixty-two "sevens," the Anointed One will be cut off and have nothing. The people of the ruler who will come will destroy the city and the Sanctuary. The end will come like a flood: War will continue until the end, and desolations have been decreed. He will confirm a covenant with many for one "seven." In the middle of the "seven" he will put an end to sacrifice and offering. And on a wing of the temple he will set up an abomination that causes desolation, until the end that is decreed is poured out on him. (NIV, Zondervan, 1985)

Through a series of calculations, it is believed that only sixty-nine of these weeks have been fulfilled (the sixty-ninth ended with the crucifixion of Jesus); thus, there is one more week or a time of seven years which has not yet taken place. It is reasoned that since it has been predicted and what has been foretold is assured of taking place, the seventieth will be also just as certain as the other sixty-nine which have already occurred. But the big question is when.

The Thessalonians passage, especially verse 17, is believed to give the conclusive evidence that there will be a taking up of all true believers in Jesus Christ at a time before the actual Second Coming occurs. I Thessalonians 4:16-17 is as follows:

> For the Lord himself will come down from heaven, with a loud command, with the voice of the archangel and with the trumpet call of God, and the dead in Christ will rise first. After that, we who are still alive and are left will be caught up together with them in the clouds to meet the Lord in the air. And so we will be with the Lord forever. (NIV, Zondervan, 1985)

The Greek word *harpazo* can mean to "to take away" or "to catch up." These two passages, Daniel 9 and I Thessalonians 4, are believed to be connected. It is claimed that the sixty-nine weeks or 483 years have already occurred. It is believed that God is outside of time, but in his own special timing, he has allowed a time period of about two thousand years to occur between the sixty-ninth and seventieth weeks. The beginning of the seventy weeks is thought to have been with the decree to rebuild the wall of Jerusalem in 445 B.C. as recorded in Nehemiah 2, and the sixty-ninth week ended with the death of Christ.

So what about this final week or seven years? There are many who believe what is called the pretribulational rapture. This view says that the saints will be caught up before the beginning of the seventieth week or the seven years of tribulation on earth. Believers in Christ will not go through this time when the Antichrist will have authority. The seven-year period is believed to be a time of terror and evil as personified in one man— Antichrist, or one who is the opposite of Christ. The belief is that this man will gain power through lies and political maneuvering. Eventually nothing will be possible without his permission. He is the ultimate 666, and all will need a special code from him in order to do anything, whether it is purchasing any item at the store or going online. This person is believed to be so smooth and enticing that he is the type who could sell freezers to Eskimos. But his heart is evil, and he is the epitome of evil. He will be responsible for the death of millions. Hitler, Stalin, Mussolini, and the fundamental Islamic terrorists pale in comparison to the devastation he will achieve when it comes to the taking of lives. Without doubt, it is a horrible time overflowing with violence and bloodshed.

Those who are caught up are seen as being spared from this time; they will be with Jesus Christ and the other saints. But those who have rejected Christ are believed to enter into this period without hope unless they too will accept Jesus by faith alone. But obviously, it will be much more difficult to do this. For one thing, it means almost certain death, especially if one lets others know of his or her decision. The Antichrist will view this as the ultimate betrayal of his authority and will swiftly and certainly kill many who reject him and receive Christ. The belief is that this will result in unimaginable horror and the loss of inestimable lives.

There are some who believe that this Rapture will not happen until after the seven-year period is completed, and this is usually called the posttribulational view. Christians will not be taken out before the beginning of this time of horror, but they will actually live through it. Many will be killed, but it is also believed that many will be supernaturally protected during these seven years. Sometimes examples are given such as the protection of Noah and his family or the many instances of supernatural protection of the apostles. Many who are posttribulational do not believe in a rapture but only a second coming. But others who are postribulationalists believe that the two events, the Rapture and Second Coming, occur very close to one another—perhaps separated only by a few days, hours, or less. The major biblical passage which is believed to teach the posttribulational rapture is I Thessalonians 1:4-10:

> For we know, brothers, loved by God, that he has chosen you, because our gospel came to you not simply with words, but also with power, with the Holy Spirit and with deep conviction. You know how we lived among you for your sake. You became imitators of us and of the Lord; in spite of severe suffering, you welcomed the message with joy given by the Holy Spirit. And so you became a model to all believers in Macedonia and Achaia. The Lord's message rang out from you not only in Macedonia and Achaia—your faith in God has become known everywhere. Therefore we do not need to say anything about it, for they themselves report what kind of reception you gave us. They will tell how you turned to God from idols to serve the living and true

God, and to wait for his Son from heaven, whom he raised from the dead—
Jesus, who rescues us from the coming wrath. (NIV, Zondervan, 1985)

Those who believe in the posttribulational Rapture place the release
of Christians from persecution at the posttribulational return of Christ.
Since release comes with the Second Coming and release from persecution is associated with the Rapture, the Rapture has to be at the same
time as the Second Coming. Those who are pretribulational believe that
this release occurred seven years previously.

The view that there will be a rapture of the saints before the Second
Coming of Christ is one of many controversial topics of theology. The
argument usually runs something like this. The belief in the rapture is a
new idea. The belief is roughly 200 years old, and any doctrine which is
not at least a thousand years old is considered new! The argument
against the Rapture continues with statements that it is not found in the
early, medieval, or Reformation church; therefore, it is highly suspect.
Since it is not the purpose of this book to attempt to explain systemat-
ic theology, there is no need to go into all the arguments for and against
the belief in a rapture. However, more information will be given in chapter two. If one interprets the Bible in a plain, word-for-word, literal way,
there is a high probability one will come to the conclusion that there is
a rapture of the saints before the actual second return of Christ.

The Tribulation Period

Many understand the seven-year period of tribulation to be a future event. But Swindoll and Jeremiah claim that Christians will not go through this period, as they will be taken out before this occurrence. They base their conclusions on the Old Testament passages of Daniel 9:24-27. It is believed according to this line of interpretation that the New Testament books of Matthew 24 and 2 Thessalonians 2 refer to the same order of events. Matthew 24 speaks of corpses, great fear, and the need to be looking for the Messiah who is coming soon. The Thessalonian passages give some detail about the "man of lawlessness" and how many will follow him.

The Great Tribulation is the period known as Daniel's seventieth week (Daniel 9:24-27). The final week, or seven-year period, many believe, is proved by the fact that it was exactly 69 x 7 years (483) between the order to rebuild Jerusalem and the cutting off (or death) of the Messiah. The remaining seventieth "week" of years belongs to Israel's age and will be characterized by the same general conditions as found in the past Jewish age as seen in the Old Testament. The present time is referred to as the period of grace or the church age and is believed to be an intercalary period that began in Acts 2 and continues until the Rapture itself. But according to Matthew 24:22, the seventieth week is shortened a little. Many believe that the term "Great Tribulation" refers to the last three and one half years specifically, which will be a time of intense persecution especially for those who

22

receive the Messiah during this period. This period has several characteristics including the following:

1. The removal of the Holy Spirit together with the Church or Christians from the earth (2 Thessalonians 2:7).

2. The casting of Satan into the earth, thus restricting him to the earth (Revelation 9-12).

3. The development of sin which had been restrained previously (2Thessalonians 2:11.

4. The rule of the man of sin (John 5:43).

5. Termination by the Second Coming of Christ, the Battle of Armageddon, and the smiting stone of Daniel 2, which is identified as Christ.

It is believed that the tribulation period, especially the last three and one half years, will be a time of persecution aimed primarily at the Jews. Perhaps the Jews have been the targets of racism more than any other racial group. All one has to do is study their history, and it is obvious that they have been horribly persecuted throughout the centuries. The twentieth century alone witnessed the murder of millions of Jewish people. Adolph Hitler and the Nazis, it is believed, were responsible for at least six million deaths alone. But some biblical scholars believe that the tribulation period will be even more devastating for the Jewish people. Judaism has never accepted Jesus Christ as the promised Messiah. The three branches of this major world religion, Orthodox, Reformed and Conservative, continue to strongly denounce any idea that Jesus is both divine and human. He is believed to have been a good person, a teacher, and an example of how to live but certainly not God the Son as Christians believe. Many believe that this will be a time of purging for Israel primarily because of her perpetual rejection of Jesus as God's Son. This purging will result into many Jewish people accepting Jesus Christ as the true Messiah, and they will be able to enter the kingdom on earth, which will last one thousand years. This time of "Jacob's trouble" (Jeremiah 30:4-7, Daniel 12:1 and Matthew 24:21) will be the last great persecution which the Jewish people will endure.

The "time of the Gentiles" will finally be over. According to Swindoll and others, this time began with the Babylonian captivity, was put on hold with the forming of the church as recorded in the New Testament book of Acts, chapter 2 and then will be revived again with the seventieth week of Daniel or during the seven-year period of tribulation on earth.

Armageddon

The Greek word *armageddon* comes from two Hebrew words, *har* and *megiddo*, which means "hill of Megiddo." Historically, the location is significant. Israelite victories and defeats occurred there, and at this location were two significant events. The location on the southern portion of the plain of Esdraelon subsequently came to be known as

Palestine's great battlefield. This is the location where Gideon defeated the Midianites as well as the site where King Saul was killed. Armageddon has come to be a poetic word depicting a horrific and final conflict. Today, even secular television commentators use the word. During the Gulf War Crisis, when scud missiles were being fired from Iraq to Israel, many newspersons were making such statements as, "Is this the beginning of Armageddon?" The word has been adopted into the vernacular of our language to refer to a cataclysmic, final battle. Many believe that this final conflict will involve several Middle Eastern countries including Iraq, Iran, and Israel. The two forces in conflict with one another will be the returning Lord and His saints against the Gentile world powers which are under the control of the Antichrist. Ultimately the forces of evil will be vanquished by Christ. This is such an antithetical view of Jesus who is typically seen as meek and mild. But this view of the conquering Christ is rooted in Old Testament prophecy, which gives a two-fold prediction. One perspective is that He will be a servant and the other that He will be the ultimate conqueror.

The writer of the book of Revelation, the Apostle John, receives divine insight into events which will occur in the future. He himself does not know the time when what he receives from God will actually take place; he simply writes as the Spirit of God impresses His thoughts on his own mind and will. John details the great battle from Revelation 16:13-16. This battle ends the times of the Gentiles, and the battle is frequently referred to as "the day of the Lord."

25

Chafer, Swindoll and Jeremiah are not alone in these particular beliefs about the subject of the end. Historically there have been many others who held to similar views such as the following: D.L. Moody, C.I. Scofield, G. Campbell Morgen, William Pettingill, Eric Sauer, and H.A. Ironside. In current times many theologians and popular preachers also believe as did Chafer.

The Second Coming

Christ's Second Coming is a belief that has been in Christian teaching since the first century. There are many New Testament passages which give the promise of His return. Perhaps one of the best-known is Revelation 22:20, the second to the last verse in the Bible, "Yes, I am coming quickly." The Greek word for quickly can also be translated "soon." It is believed that Jesus gave these words sometime before 30 A.D. That means close to 2,000 years have lapsed. One thing is certain; there must be a difference in the way in which humans and God look at time!

The belief in the Second Coming is considered an essential belief in Christianity—the Catholic, Protestant, and Eastern Orthodox Churches all believe that this event will occur. With the return of Jesus Christ, it is believed that the curse which has plagued humanity and the earth will finally be lifted. There will be either eternal connection or separation from God.

The Second Coming of Jesus Christ is the event which announces the beginning of His one-thousand year earthly reign. This will be a period of near perfection on earth. All the attempts which human beings have concocted to produce a utopia have failed miserably, but this one will have no glitches. Finally, all which is wrong about humanity will be corrected. It is believed that only those who belong to Christ will enter the kingdom—only the spiritually righteous have the privilege of reigning with Him. Those who have rejected Christ, who have not placed saving faith in Him, will not be allowed to enter. It is believed that since there will be no sin during this time, people will not die; they will live in their bodies for the entire duration of the period.

At the first advent of Christ, from His birth until His death and resurrection, the kingdom was not fully established. Jesus certainly did preach, as did John the Baptist, about the kingdom. But it is believed that because of Jesus' death, the kingdom plans had to be put on hold. This does not mean though that a foretaste of the kingdom did not happen. After all, the New Testament Gospels are chock-full of accounts of how Jesus cast out demons, healed many, and raised people from the dead! Even the Apostles were given great power and authority as they were able to do the same. But the promised kingdom in all its fullness as promised in the Bible is lacking presently, and the belief is that only in the future from our current times will the perfected state be on earth.

The belief is that only with the literal second coming of Jesus Christ will this promised reign of Jesus truly begin. It is believed that there are seven achievements which will be consummated in the Second Coming of Jesus Christ:

1. Christ Himself returns as He left the earth, in the clouds of heaven and with power and great glory.

2. Christ takes the throne of His ancestor David, which is the throne of glory, and reigns forever.

3. Christ comes, not to a converted world but to the earth in rebellion against God and against His Messiah, and conquers it by the might of His own infinite power.

4. At Christ's coming, judgment will fall upon Israel, upon the nations, upon Satan, and upon the Man of Sin.

5. Christ's coming is accompanied by the convulsion of nature and accomplishes her release from the curse.

6. Christ's coming provokes Israel's long-predicted repentance and brings her salvation.

7. At His coming Christ establishes His kingdom of righteousness and peace with converted Jewish people regathered to their own land, united and blessed under their King" and Gentiles as another class of people, sharing in that kingdom.

The Second Coming will be a catalyst setting into action many events. Sometimes those who believe in a rapture of believers, which is to take place before the actual Second Coming, will actually use the phrase

Second Coming to refer to both the Rapture of believers and the return of Christ before the establishing of the kingdom. The Rapture occurs before the seven-year period, while the actual Second Coming occurs at the conclusion of the seven years.

The Resurrections

There are many resurrections mentioned in the Bible though many Christians believe in just one general resurrection at the end of time. Chafer believes that the various resurrections actually show a unity. The first resurrection happens at the same time as the Rapture, and the saints who have died since the time of the beginning of the Church as recorded in Acts 2 will be taken along with the living saints. Old Testament saints as well as saints who die during the tribulation period will then be resurrected at the completion of the seven-year period of tribulation; those who have accepted Christ will enter into the kingdom on earth and eventually the eternal state or heaven which commences after the one thousand-year reign. However, those who have not received Christ will experience separation from God. All of the unsaved will be resurrected at the conclusion of the one thousand-year reign of Christ, and they will face judgment at the Great White Throne Judgment.

The Bible is not too clear on just what the resurrection body is like. One thing for certain, it is not like the human bodies we now possess.

29

We can look at how the New Testament describes Jesus' resurrected body. The Scriptures say that He was able to eat after He resurrected from the dead, and He was also able to get from one place to another instantly. He also did not need a door as He is described as going through a wall in order to get into a house! About all we can say is that the limitations of the present body do not appear to be present in the resurrected body. This newly constructed body is somehow eternal! Unimaginable delights await those who are in Christ as they serve Him in those bodies in the eons of time.

The Judgments

The Bible states that there is not just one general judgment, but instead many. Chafer believes that there are in fact eight including the following: judgment of the cross, self, believers, the believers' works, Israel, the nations, angels, and unbelievers at the Great White Throne. Only three, the Judgment Seat of Christ, the Great White Throne, and Nations, are essential judgments since they portray the difference between those who are saved and those who are not.

Why is an understanding of the judgments as contained in the Bible important? The Judgment Seat of Christ, which is only for believers in Christ, gives incentive for one to live a righteous life after the salvation experience. At this judgment, one will be judged not according to his/her sins, but only according to the merits which the person has performed during his journey on earth. A correct understanding of this judgment on the part of the believer acts as an incentive for one to give of his best to the Master daily. The Great White Throne Judgment gives confidence to the child of God that he will not stand before God to have his works reviewed in a negative manner, and this last judgment is specifically for those who have rejected God's Son, Jesus Christ. The Judgment of Nations determines who will be able to live in the one thousand year reign with Christ.

There are reasons why the Judgment of the Nations has been minimally emphasized . First, there is a failure to recognize Israel and her relationship to other nations. Second, there has been a general failure to comprehend the importance of Israel as the chosen people of God. Many believe that the kingdom belongs to Israel, and only the nations who have proven themselves kindly disposed to that people are permitted to enter and share in that earthly glory.

The believer's judgment will be different from that which will take place at the Great White Throne because at this judgment, God will judge the unbeliever according to his works since all who are present at this time do not have saving faith in Jesus. The result of this judgment is eternal separation from God. Believers can stand before God as righteous because they are justified by faith, and they will never be separated from His love. It is believed that some who are in Christ may lose rewards which they could have had if they had lived in a more righteous manner after their reception of Christ. But they will not be judged in order to determine what the measure of their punishment will be. This judgment, the Judgment Seat of Christ, occurs immediately after the Rapture of the saints.

But of all the judgments, the Great White Throne is the one which is described fearfully, for there is no hope for those who undergo this experience. Many have argued that this judgment seems to make God unloving and vengeful. Without going into detail, it can easily be argued that God does not send people to hell—each one is responsible ultimately for either accepting or rejecting the Son. Possibly there are degrees of punishment, so that the person who never had the opportunity will not experience the same sense of "lostness" as the person who heard the message but yet rejected the offer. The reality of this judgment should cause a deep sense of gratitude within the heart of every true believer, but also a sense of urgency in telling others about the need to respond to the offer now. Procrastination seems to be part of human makeup, and many think somehow they can put off life's most important decision until the very last moment, but no one knows just how long God gives to each one life. It seems that for most people, there is no last conscious moment to decide to receive Christ as Saviour.

~· Chapter Two ·~

Searching Other Views: Bottom Line Conclusions

The Time of the Rapture

There is a big controversy among many who believe in the Rapture. There are some who believe they can argue that Christians must go through the seven-year period of tribulation—they will not be spared but must undergo all of the horrors of this time. Those who believe this will be the situation are called "posttribulationalists." This view states that immediately after the Rapture of the saints, the Second Coming will take place. The arguments usually go like this. The Bible nowhere teaches a secret rapture or any coming of the Lord prior to his appearing as described in the book of Revelation 19. It is said that the Rapture and the Second Coming are described by the same words. The promise to be delivered from the wrath does not mean that the Church literally will be taken out before the cruelties begin. An example which is sometimes used is the argument that as God protected the Israelites in Egypt during the plagues, so He will protect Christians during the time of tribulation. Also, it is believed that Matthew 24:22 proves saints are on the earth during the tribulation. The final view of those who are posttribulational is that the Bible only speaks of a general Second Coming of Christ and not a coming of Christ for the saints seven years before the real coming.

There are two other views of the Rapture which have also been suggested as alternatives as to when the saints will be taken out. One is called the Partial Rapture view which claims that only those who are ready and waiting for Christ will be taken up. Though a person is a believer, that individual may not be at such a spiritual state which would warrant his /her being taken; they are overly concerned by the cares of everyday living, so they forfeit their opportunity. This view claims that there will be several raptures, at least three which will occur at the beginning, mid point and end of the seven years of tribulation. There does not seem to be adequate support for this belief in the Bible. Some claim that Hebrews 9:28 is a text which supports this belief since the passage is about being prepared and eagerly waiting for His return.

VIEWS OF THE RAPTURE

PRETRIBULATIONISM

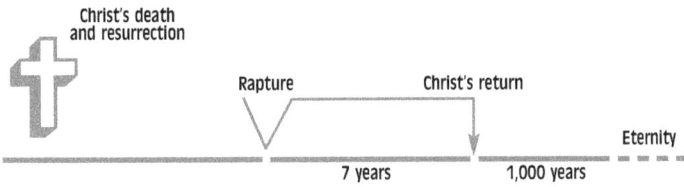

Christ's death
and resurrection

Rapture

Christ's return

Eternity

7 years

1,000 years

MIDTRIBULATIONISM

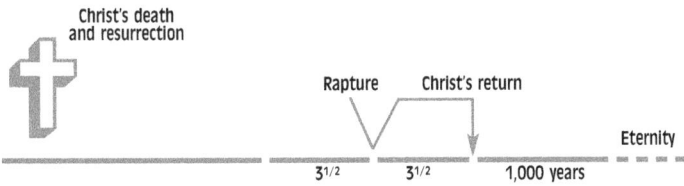

Christ's death
and resurrection

Rapture

Christ's return

Eternity

$3^{1/2}$

$3^{1/2}$

1,000 years

POSTTRIBULATIONISM

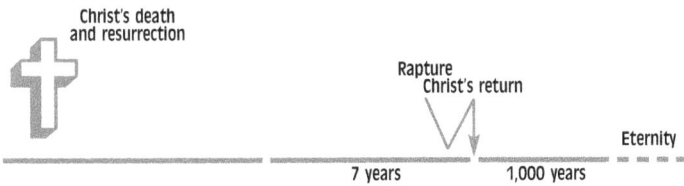

Christ's death
and resurrection

Rapture
Christ's return

Eternity

7 years

1,000 years

PARTIAL RAPTURE

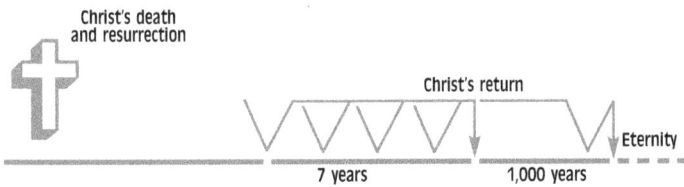

Christ's death
and resurrection

Christ's return

Eternity

7 years

1,000 years

But there is another view which appears to have more substance to it, referred to as the midtribulational view. This is the belief that the saints will be taken out before the last three and one half years of the seven-year tribulation, at which time the real period of terror on earth begins The first half (three and one half years) apparently will appear to be smooth as the Antichrist assumes power, and the world looks to this person as the embodiment of hope. But when he is able to possess total control, then the rampage will begin. This is the period of terror which the Church, believers in Jesus Christ, will not have to undergo according to this view. Those who believe in this view claim that the last trump of I Corinthians 15:52 is the same as the seventh trumpet of Revelation 11:15, and that this is sounded at the middle of the tribulation. But the strongest argument put forth is that the Great Tribulation is only the last three and one half years of the last half of Daniel's seventieth week, and the Church is promised deliverance only from this period. Revelation 11 is usually claimed to be support for this view.

The Kingdom: What Is It?

The word *Kingdom* is mentioned many times in the Bible, especially in the Gospels of Matthew, Mark, and Luke. For example, in Matthew 4:17, Jesus cried out, "Repent, for the kingdom of heaven is near." In Matthew 6:33, Jesus promised, "But seek first his kingdom and his righteousness, and all these things will be given to you as well." There have been many interpretations of just what this kingdom is and when it will occur. The New Testament was originally written in the language of Greek (a specific kind called Koine Greek), and there is a particular word used to refer to this kingdom. *Basileia* can mean reign, rule, kingdom, or domain. Many prefer to use the word millennium when they refer to the biblical concept of kingdom. The word *millennium* comes from the Latin, *mille*, which means a thousand—a thousand years of time, which has been interpreted to be an extended period of bliss and near perfection on earth. Human beings instinctively have longed for such a condition; there is a certain fascination on the part of us concerning the idea of one thousand years. Remember the excitement of the new millennium of 2000? Human beings have an innate longing for a time of completion on earth as the number 1000 in a sense represents perfection. Some of these attempts have been for evil purposes such as the Third Reich or the belief that human power exerted in an especially sinister manner can bring in this state. History is full of such failed efforts.

The key question is, when does this millennium or kingdom occur? Christians in particular have different opinions of the time and duration of this period. Some believe that the word *thousand* is only symbolic, and that the period could be much shorter, whereas others say it is simply an indefinite period, perhaps even longer than one thousand years.

One very common view today claims that only with the personal coming of Jesus Christ will the millennium be established. The argument goes something like this. It is true that humankind is much more advanced than in previous decades and centuries; medicine, science, technology, and education are at the highest level ever. This fact is generally recognized globally. But the major problem is that human beings are not getting better morally because wars, terrorism, and crimes continue to escalate. In fact, many make the case that it appears human nature is actually becoming more and more corrupt. How can we possibly say that the world is getting better and eventually humanity will usher in a glorious period where all of the above problems will no longer be with us?

This view believes that the promise the kingdom will occur is grounded in various agreements between God and people in the Bible, and two covenants are seen as highly significant. These two covenants are interpreted to be unconditional; that is, they will take place since God has declared that they will. God made a promise with Abraham, and this is usually referred to as the Abrahamic Covenant. In Genesis 12, God told Abraham that he would be a great nation and blessed of God and even that all people on earth would be blessed through this nation. Many understand that this nation is the Jewish people and that the ultimate blessing would come through Jesus Christ, God in the flesh.

The other covenant or promise which God made was with King David, and this is found in 2 Samual 7. Here the promise to David is that one who is in his line will reign forever and will establish an eternal kingdom. Many interpret this to refer ultimately to Jesus Christ, who is

41

said to be the Son of David in the New Testament. This promise which was made to David over three thousand years ago will eventually be fulfilled in none other than God's Son, Jesus, who is believed to have come to earth, lived, died, resurrected and ascended back to the Father.

This group also believes that there are two major teachings of Christ concerning times future to Him and these are referred to as the Olivet Discourse and the Sermon on the Mount. Many believe that the Olivet Discourse pertains to the time of tribulation on earth. However, it is believed that both discourses are addressed to Israel.

The Olivet Discourse is found in Matthew 24 and 25, and the message begins with a description of the tribulation period and concludes with the judgments which will fall upon Israel and then all nations. This group believes that the gospel of the kingdom will be preached during the time of seven years of tribulation on earth. The Olivet Discourse speaks of judgment upon Israel and the Lord's coming in glory with angels. His coming will mark the end of the time of tribulation, and the next major event to occur is the thousand-year reign of Jesus.

The Sermon on the Mount is the second most important prophetic message which Jesus spoke according to this view. This message is found in Matthew 5-7, and it is believed that the primary application is not to this present time but in the future thousand-year period. The entire message is one of blessedness or the absence of strife and any condition which would not be conducive to supreme happiness.

John the Baptist announced with great vigor the coming of the kingdom and fulfilled the prophetic words of Isaiah 40:3, which states: "A voice is calling, clear the way for the Lord in the wilderness; make smooth in the desert a highway for our God." It is believed that John came preaching a literal, earthly one thousand year reign which Jesus himself will establish. This kingdom message was also offered by Jesus Christ, and Israel as a nation rejected this offer. The message will again be offered to the same people, and if accepted, they will be allowed to enter the kingdom, or the period of one thousand years of peace and prosperity on earth.

Only those who have survived the seven-year period of tribulation and have been judged as sheep, those who are spiritually related to Christ, will be allowed to enter the kingdom or period of one-thousand years of peace on earth. It is believed that there are actually two classes of people at the Judgment of the Nations: the sheep and the goats. The sheep are those who spiritually belong to God, while the goats are those who have rejected God, specifically Jesus Christ. Gentiles will also be allowed to enter the kingdom, but only those who have a personal relationship with Jesus. Two key words in the kingdom period are *righteousness* and *peace*. The King will reign with an iron hand, evil will be punished immediately, and all the forms of evil will be judged in perfect righteousness. There is seen to be five characteristics of the kingdom: (1) the kingdom will be God-ruled; (2) it will be heavenly in character; (3) the kingdom will be over regathered and converted Israel; (4) it will be established by the returning King; (5) the reign will be spiritual. In

43

summary, the King will reign over His people, and His authority will be unquestioned.

Satan is to be bound at the beginning of the millennial reign; therefore, he cannot entice the saints. The New Testament in the book of Revelation 20:2 speaks of the binding of Satan for one thousand years. There will be a limited amount of crime and evil during this period since the main instigator is not able to tempt people. It is believed though the believers are still in their earthly bodies, which are supernaturally able to live at least one thousand years, and since they live in the flesh, they are still at times subject to its desires. But at least they cannot say, "The devil made me do it!" The Bible does not give too much information about what the condition of the environment will be during the millennial reign of Christ. Some Old Testament passages are believed to allude to this period such as Isaiah 11:6-9, which refers to the subduing of the animal kingdom and that everyone on earth will know the Lord. If interpreted literally, Isaiah 55:12-13 speaks of the absence of thorns and briars. Micah 4:3 anticipates a time when the nations will no longer be involved in war. The promise of God's total forgiveness of the sins of Israel is promised in Jeremiah 31:33-34. The millennium is a time of peace.

The thousand-year reign of Christ will close with specific and cataclysmic events, specifically with the release of Satan . Many believe literally Revelation 20:7-8 which states:

VIEWS OF THE KINGDOM

POSTMILLENNIAL VIEW OF THE KINGDOM
(KINGDOM BEFORE THE SECOND COMING)

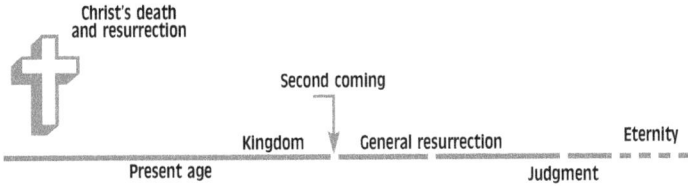

Christ's death
and resurrection

Second coming

Kingdom   General resurrection   Eternity

Present age   Judgment

AMILLENNIAL VIEW OF THE KINGDOM
(KINGDOM PRESENT NOW)

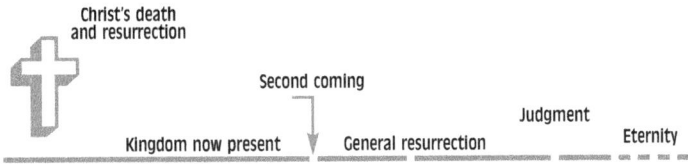

Christ's death
and resurrection

Second coming

Judgment

Kingdom now present   General resurrection   Eternity

DISPENSATIONAL PREMILLENNIAL VIEW
(KINGDOM IN THE FUTURE)

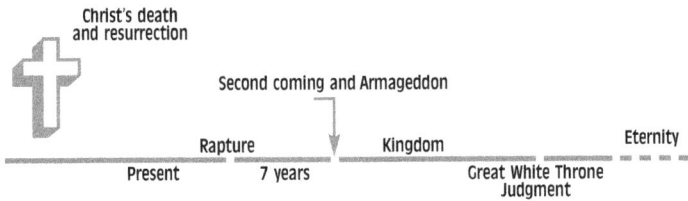

Christ's death
and resurrection

Second coming and Armageddon

Rapture   Kingdom   Eternity

Present   7 years   Great White Throne
Judgment

45

And when the thousand years are completed, Satan will be released from his prison, and will come out to deceive the nations which are in the corners of the earth, God and Magog, to gather them together for the war; and the number of them is like the sand on the seashore.(NIV, Zondervan, 1985)

Satan is the cause behind a final battle which many refer to as Gog and Magog. As individuals are pressured to engage in sin, so Satan causes unrest among the mass of humanity inciting them to kill those belonging to other nations.

It is believed that Revelation 21 depicts that the present order of the earth and heavens will pass away. The final resurrection and the Great White Throne Judgment are for those who are not spiritually related to Jesus Christ; their judgment along with Satan and his other fallen angels will result in eternal banishment from the presence of God. A new heaven and earth will be created according to Revelation 21:1. Heaven is described as a place indescribably beautiful and without tears, pain, death and darkness.

Some believe that Jesus will withdraw as King at the end of the thousand-year reign and use I Corinthians 15:24-28 to support this. Others believe that Jesus will reign eternally on the throne, but of course under the ultimate authority of God the Father.

Other Views of the Kingdom

Premillennialism, or the belief that Jesus will come before the kingdom can be set up, dates back to the first century. This was the view of the early Church, though there was no idea of a secret rapture of the saints until the middle of the nineteenth century. Those who do not believe in premillennialism are quick to say that it is a negative view of what is happening in the world. Many times they are accused of being negative thinkers. The view does say it is going to get worse before it will get better! But many say it is simply a realistic view of the way everything in the twenty-first century is unfolding. The AIDS virus will probably continue to spread and mutate taking innumerable lives, wars are seemingly on the increase, and economic uncertainties appear to be getting worse; racism will always be with us, but Jesus' coming will correct all of these problems according to premillennialism, or the view which states Jesus will come before the kingdom.

The Kingdom before the Second Coming

There is another view which was very popular in America in the latter part of the nineteenth century until about 1940, which is called postmillennialism. This position says that humanity, especially the saints, will be the ones who along with God's help, will assure that the kingdom will eventually come to pass. John Whitby (1638-1726, British preacher) is widely recognized as the originator of this particular view of the millennium. About two hundred years ago, theologians and pastors, in America especially, continued to write and speak about the power of the gospel of Jesus Christ, and that through technology the gospel would be brought to all parts of the world soon. The millennium was said to be a golden age on earth where especially spiritual prosperity ruled. Not every evil would necessarily be destroyed but would be held in check by the power of the Church of Jesus Christ. This kingdom, it was believed, would continue to come slowly. The technological advances of the late nineteenth century seemed to be a foretaste of such a kingdom. This kingdom was believed to be not one of earthly or political splendor, but it would consist of righteousness, peace, and joy. The condition for admission to the kingdom was believed to be regeneration or receiving the person of Christ personally.

How did it happen that such a view became popular? The technological progress of the times had something to do with it. But also a group of very influential theologians from predominately Princeton Theological Seminary began to strongly promote this view. Charles Hodge, a professor at Princeton, influenced many concerning this view. About fifty years ago, Loraine Boettner through his writings influenced many to accept this view. Instead of interpreting the prophecies in a literal way as the premillennialists did, they looked at them in more of a symbolic and figurative manner. Revelation 20 would be fulfilled in the earthly kingdom that is brought in by the Church's efforts.

49

This view gradually disappeared. World War I, which was supposedly the war to end all wars, only escalated to more wars on the horizon, especially in Europe. The Great Depression in America showed millions of people that they could not trust the economic system or their bank accounts. World War II, with its horrific devastation taking over fifty million lives and destroying cities and countries, showed the world that something is desperately twisted about human nature. Postmillennialism, or the belief that humans could bring in a perfected order, was no longer seen as viable.

However, in the past ten years, this view has made somewhat of a resurgence. R.C. Sproul, a well-known contemporary author and speaker, continues to promote this view. Remember that this understanding of the kingdom is not the same as those who believe that Jesus will come before the kingdom and will establish the millennium through His own personal presence. Rather, the postmillennial view states that the Gospel is so powerful and pervasive that eventually the immoral structures of society and a huge number of people will genuinely receive Jesus Christ; thus, His reign will be established on earth. Many argue that this view does not fit reality as it appears that wars are increasing and various diseases continue to escalate. Also, the Apostle Paul wrote in 2 Timothy 3:1-5 that in the last days men will be inhumane and lovers of pleasure more than lovers of God. Also, Jesus stated as recorded in Matthew 7:13-14, that few, not many, will find and live a righteous life. Many argue, then, that the teachings of the Bible do not supature.

The Kingdom Present Now

This is the majority view of Christians concerning the interpretation of the thousand-year reign of Jesus Christ. Most main-line Protestant denominations in America, the Orthodox Church and the Roman Catholic Church hold to this view. It was none other than Augustine (354-420 A.D, philosopher and theologian) who first proposed this view. The kingdom to him meant that Christ's reign is now occurring in the hearts or spirits of all true Christians. Of course, during his time there was only one church, the Roman Catholic Church. The many denominations within Christianity such as Baptist, Methodist, Presbyterian, Episcopalian and Lutheran would not emerge until the sixteenth and subsequent centuries. Two well-known Protestant representatives of this view are Steve Brown and Wayne Grudem. Other theologians who believe that this is the correct understanding of the kingdom are the following: George Ladd, Anthony Hoekema and Louis Berkhof.

The amillennial position is not as complicated as the dispensational premillennial. This view claims that the Second Coming of Jesus Christ could occur at any moment. A belief in a rapture before the Second Coming is not part of this scheme as amillennialists believe that the I Thessalonians 4 passage is referring to the Second Coming and not to a secret rapture of the saints before the Second Coming. There is no future seven-year period of tribulation as that terrible period is believed to have already taken place in the time of the first century when so many Christians were persecuted in the Roman Empire under such emperors as Nero.

Crucial to the understanding of the amillennial approach is the belief that Satan was bound at the first coming of Christ. It is often claimed that the only place where the thousand-year reign is found in the Bible is in Revelation 20, and this period probably is more symbolic than literal. Since Satan has been bound, the kingdom exists now. Even though this position says Satan is now bound, this does not mean that he does not have any power. Satan's ultimate defeat was at the cross when Jesus died, and then His resurrection from the dead and ascension back to the Father in heaven confirm that righteousness is the victor. There may be evil present now, but it is constantly being checked by the power of God. It is because of Satan's binding that the gospel can be preached throughout the world, though there is still great opposition. It is believed that his binding makes missions and evangelism possible. Many who oppose this view sometimes say if Satan is bound then he must have a very long and light chain! Those who believe in amillennialism say that Revelation 20 describes the scene of souls in heaven during the period between the first and second comings of Christ or from the first century to the present. This is what is happening in heaven right now.

This view does say that the Second Coming will be preceded by various signs, such as the preaching of the gospel to every nation, the conversion of Israel, and some would add that great tribulation will take place before Christ's coming. These signs are said to have been present from the beginning of the Christian era to the present. According to the amillennial position, the Second Coming of Christ will be a single event, and at His coming there will be a general resurrection of both unbelievers and believers. After the judgment the eternal state will begin.

The Kingdom after the Second Coming

Lewis Sperry Chafer did not just invent his views about the future. He spent many years of study before he reached his conclusions. There were many influences upon his understanding of the future. He was a man of great spiritual discernment, and he became convinced that through prayer and Bible study the truth about the future would unfold for him. Although he associated for many years with dispensationalists, and read hundreds of theologians who held to this system, he came to his conclusions concerning the future by independent study. He interpreted the Bible in a plain manner; that is, according to basic rules of grammar and plain, word-for-word interpretation.

Why does he believe so strongly in premillennialism? He believes in approaching the Scriptures in a literal manner—understanding the words as they are written. Of course, this does not mean Chafer does not believe that the Bible has figures of speech and symbols. But to him their interpretation is subject to a plain, literal method of interpretation.

Throughout his life, Chafer was a man who believed that the Holy

Spirit is able to reveal the true meaning of the Bible. For example, to interpret as accurately as possible the Bible, he believes it is very helpful to know the original languages of the Bible, Hebrew and Greek. He believes that at least 20 percent of the Bible contained prophetic themes, or those topics which were future from the time of the original writing.

There are seven major themes of prophecy in the Old Testament, and these include prophecy concerning the Gentiles, Israel's early history, the nation itself, Israel's last dispersion and regathering, the advent of the Messiah, the Great Tribulation, and Messiah's kingdom on earth. The New Testament also has themes concerning prophecy, namely prophecy concerning the present age, the divine purpose of the calling out of the Church from both Jews and Gentiles, the Great Tribulation, Satan and the forces of evil, the Second Coming of Christ, the Messianic kingdom, and the eternal state or heaven.

Chafer speaks of ten major highways of prophecy traced through the Bible. These are the Lord Jesus Christ, the Church, the resurrection and the Rapture of the saints, the Great Tribulation, Satan and evil, the Antichrist, the course and end of apostate Christendom, the beginning, extenuation and end of the Gentile times, the Second Coming of Christ, and Israel's covenants.

Many other people did influence his views about the future. Perhaps the most significant person was C. I. Scofield, the author of the Scofield Reference Bible. This one-time practicing lawyer entered the ministry after his conversion experience and devoted years to a personal study of the theme of the future in both the Old and New Testaments. Chafer said and wrote on many occasions that Scofield was like a father to him. Their views on the future are almost identical. But there were others who impacted his conclusions. The Anglican theologian, W.H. Griffith Thomas, also influenced Chafer's views of the future. George N.H. Peters, a Lutheran pastor, wrote a book called *The Theocratic Kingdom*; and in this work he states that Israel will once again be a nation, the Antichrist's reign is future as well as the Battle of Armageddon. Chafer also read widely the works of various professors at Princeton Theological Seminary such as A. A. Hodge, Charles Hodge, and B.B. Warfield. Chafer was a Presbyterian minister, and he agreed with the writings of these professors. But he noticed that they did not have much if anything to say about the future, and they even admitted that they felt inadequate when it came to determining what the Bible claims concerning the future.

One fascinating relationship was that between Chafer and H.A. Ironside, the pastor of the Moody Church in Chicago. Chafer in many of his books states his agreement with Ironside's interpretation of Daniel seven. Both believe that this chapter predicts not only the Medo-Persian, Greek and Roman empires, but also a fourth kingdom, whose empire they believe is still future. It is the same empire mentioned in Revelation 13, which is the kingdom of the Antichrist. Chafer and Ironside both believe that the saints, or those who have received Jesus as personal Saviour, will not experience the terror of this period. They will be raptured before this empire comes to power. We have seen a dramatic shift of power and interest in recent years. In previous decades, it was believed that Europe was the real powerhouse. I can remember how the older generation would say, "Anything that comes out of Germany will impact the world." While Germany and other European countries are very influential, it appears that the Middle East is growing quickly in political and economic strength. Chafer understood this many years before Israel became a nation and countries such as Iran, Iraq and Afghanistan began to assert their dominance. With the continuing war on terrorism, we are reminded that there will always be uneasy relations between those who are Christians and Muslims. Those who are of the Islamic faith adamantly state that Jesus was a great prophet, but certainly not God the Son as Christians believe. The world has yet to see where the war on terrorism will lead us.

KINGDOM BOUND: OUR JOURNEY OF JOY

Part Two

~· Chapter Three ·~

Preparing Now:
Living in the Present and the Future

When a person understands the certainty of Christ's definite reign and sovereignty over the future, then the believer can confidently travel this life with joy. The Bible offers wonderful, practical guidelines about how a person can live not only a successful life, but also one which is meaningful; those who disagree with this have either not entered into a relationship with God or have not grown once they have commenced the journey. Eternity with God is a promise, but there is also help along the way. For many, the Bible is somewhat like a dusty book, good for the grandparents and the older generation, but totally irrelevant to the post-modern generation. There are at least ten qualities which are found in the 1100 chapters of the Bible which many believe are helpful in their lives. Some people have more of these qualities and in a greater measure than others, and certainly I would not say that these are the only ones which are needed.

All of us know of that almost magical-like person, one who exudes charm, charisma, poise and is just a pleasure to be around. Perhaps you have even thought to yourself, "Wouldn't it be great to be like that person?" The good new is that you can! Of course, you will still be you, but the best you possible. Let us journey and look at some qualities the Bible promotes, which can enhance our lives.

Preparing:

I remember as a boy scout, we were told that the motto was, "Be prepared." Somehow as an eight-year-old, all that was involved with that motto did not sink in. In every discipline, preparation is essential. Sometimes we listen to a great musician and think that person was born that way, but we are unaware of all of the years of labor and preparation, which these talented people have devoted to their profession.

In I Peter 1:13, the apostle writes, "Therefore, prepare your minds for action." It has been said that the greatest battle is that for one's mind. Surely many would say that it is the war in Iraq, but what goes on in the thinking of a person ultimately impacts actions, deeds, and the destiny of each person. In a sense, each one of us holds our destiny in our own hands. The Bible does teach that there is a God who is sovereign and in control of all issues and events; I believe this totally. On the other hand, we can make decisions, and all of us do. Even the small decisions we make every day eventually add up and determine who and what we will be and become. Someone has said that each person's destiny can be traced to a thought, which becomes an action, this becomes a habit which can control the direction of a person's life, and thus, one's destiny.

When I was a child, my mother told me that no achievement of worth happens without a great amount of effort. In effect, she was saying that preparation is necessary in every aspect of life. There is a sense though that we will never feel totally prepared, no matter how much time and effort we have put into a given exercise or a particular event. There is always that fear of what if, or maybe my opponent or situation will be stronger than I. The more prepared we are, the more such feelings are minimized, and we are able to carry on our responsibilities with a greater degree of confidence and joy. Ask God to help you become a person who prepares for the large as well as the small issues in life. I still have the letter which my grandfather sent to me on my tenth birthday. He closed by quoting to me the King James Version of Proverbs 3:5-6, "Trust in the Lord with all thine heart; and lean not unto thine own understanding. In all thy ways acknowledge him, and he shall direct they paths." That in many ways says it all! Ask for God's wisdom, and you will never be disappointed. Such preparation will prevent a person years later saying to himself and others, "If only," or "I could have, should have, or would have."

Praying:

Real prayer involves many facets of one's life. Many people think in terms of prayer as something to engage in order to receive something. It is true; that is part of prayer but perhaps should not be considered the highest motivation. It seems that prayer is primarily a means by which we mere mortals can praise a loving, all-powerful and knowing God for loving us and allowing us to enter into communication with Him. Most know what is commonly called "The Lord's Prayer," which is found in Matthew 6:9-13. Jesus tells his disciples to begin this prayer with honoring the name of God and praying that His will be done. For those who are in a personal relationship with God through His Son, praying such a prayer glorifies and honors God. After all, we are here not to glorify ourselves but to seek and do His will.

Meaningful prayer is not easy. The Bible even instructs us to pray for our enemies, and the implication is to pray for good in their lives. How many people do you know who truly even entertain such a thought?

Medical doctors have known for a long time that there is a relationship between those who engage in sincere prayer and those who do not. Statistics and individual testimonies attest to the fact that those who pray on a regular basis have a greater chance of experiencing less anxiety, lower blood pressure, and all-around good health.

We should first give our heart-felt adoration and love toward God. The more we do this, the less we focus on ourselves, and we will begin to realize that life is not all about us; we are not the center of the universe. It is amazing how this lifts a giant burden off of a person. We should also confess our shortcomings, even our sins, to use a word which so many think is old fashioned. When I was in fifth grade, I threw a spit ball, and the teacher asked who did it. (She had a good idea it was I.) She looked at me with her beady eyes, and said, "Confession is good for the soul!" I did confess, and yes, I did feel better. Many people are piling up day after day, year after year unconfessed issues. No wonder so many are having physical and emotional troubles. David in Psalm 51:2 wrote: "Wash me thoroughly from my iniquity, and cleanse me from my sin."

The person who knows that she or he is forgiven can live life to the fullest. God has forgiven him/her and that person is in a position now to forgive himself and others.

Meditating:

Have you ever read something and at the completion could not exactly say what it was that you had just read? Maybe it was something short, requiring only a few minutes of reading or longer, perhaps several hours. It could be that you were tired or distracted, but it could also be that you had not engaged in a measure of meditation. Webster tells us that the word means, "to engage in contemplation or reflection; to plan or project in the mind."

In the first Psalm, verses 1-3 we read,

> Blessed is the man who does not walk in the counsel of the wicked or stand in the way of sinners or sit in the seat of mockers. But his delight is in the law of the Lord, and on his law he meditates day and night. He is like a tree planted by streams of water, which yields its fruit in season and whose leaf does not wither, whatever he does prospers. (NIN, Zondervan, 1985)

This is the God's promise to His people. Something wonderful begins to happen when a person engages in meditation in a manner prescribed by the Lord.

I was raised in Minnesota where my father was a veterinarian. I recall as a child seeing a cow which looked like it was chewing bubble gum. She was lying in a pasture, looking quite content chewing on and on. My father told me that she was "chewing her cud." Another word for this expression is "ruminating," which refers to chewing something again which had been first only slightly chewed. It takes time for the cow,

66

which looks as if she has all the time in world! You and I actually have more time than we think. Under the pressure of moment, we are very capable of using the honorable excuse, "I don't have time." The fact is, if one plans, he/she will have more than enough time.

Meditating implies rethinking an issue. Sometimes it might mean putting something out of mind for a period and then coming back to the issue a day or two latter or even longer. We know that the mind works on issues over which we are concerned on a subconscious level. This is why it is so important to fill our minds with good thoughts right before we doze off every night. During the period we are sleeping, the mind is still at work and what has concerned us especially before sleep will continue to play itself over and over again while we are not aware of it. If you have an issue with which you are concerned, go over it again perhaps an hour before bedtime, and you may be amazed when you awake to have the answer which you were searching for from a recent or past issue.

A person skilled in meditation is able to see all the angles, or at least more than he could before becoming a meditator. Of course, there is always the problem of meditating and never coming to a solid conclusion. Some have termed this, "analysis paralysis." Meditation will help a person see contingencies, or the "what ifs" of something which is causing concern. We have all seen on the T.V. or movies the coach diagramming for the football team various plays. These plans apply to the offensive as well as the defensive line. Each player becomes aware of the possible challenges as well as the opportunities by attempting to speculate what could happen. It also helps if they know something about the other team and individual players. I believe that our lives would be much more meaningful if we would take some time and do such planning each day.

The end result of meditating is applying; theory without application means that the knowledge is not rooted in reality. Every major profession has an internship for those who are attempting to become proficient. For example, doctors must undergo years of experience in an internship. Ideally, they work alongside those who are more experienced and competent in what they do. The doctor is able to see various cases and gradually more responsibility is shifted to the intern. Previously for years, the intern had read about various medical problems and procedures and understood the theory, but now with practical, hands on experience, he understands what he read in another dimension.

What should a person meditate upon? Pick a portion of scripture from the Bible, perhaps only one verse or several. Read them again and again until you have them memorized. One of my favorite verses is Galatians 5:22, which states, "But the fruit of the Spirit is love, joy, peace, patience, kindness, goodness, faithfulness, gentleness and self control. Against such there is no law." There are nine key qualities which every person should ideally possess. Think about what love means to you. Perhaps a loving person or other synonyms of the particular word come to mind. Do that with the other eight; you may take one for an entire day or even a week. By the time you complete the nine, you will have grown in awareness and application of each one of these wonderful attributes. They will become part of you, and more than likely people will comment that they see these qualities in your life.

Possessing the Highest Motive:

Let's face it, many times we do things for all the wrong motives. When we start to question our motives, it is easy to become discouraged. I knew one person who really was loving and caring, and I asked him about this wonderful quality. He replied that he was such a person because, "It feels good to be kind to others." It would be possible to interpret what he did and said to mean that really he was thinking about his own self interest and how to please himself.

Ask the average person why he or she engages in a certain activity or profession, and more than likely, you will hear something about money, recognition, or personal fulfillment. I do not know if it is possible in this life to have perfect motives. Even parental love is sometimes tinged with selfish motives. If you have ever witnessed an irate parent fly off the handle at the referee, a player, or another parent at an athletic contest, then you begin to realize that behind all that anger might be less than perfect motives. The parent could be vicariously playing the game himself through the child and becoming angry and rude when things do not go his way.

Some people when they realize their motives are not pure actually become depressed. Others begin the fine art of judging their opponent's motives. I knew a young lady who when she would become angry with someone would begin her attack with such words as, "The reason you are saying that is because ...." She was attempting to read the motives of the other person.

When in graduate school, my professor, who was a Christian psychiatrist, was lecturing on this topic. He said that it might be good not to worry about our motives since they never will be totally pure. All we can do is our best. A well-known preacher from many years ago, Donald Grey Barnhouse, said that he could hardly wait to get to heaven because then he would have pure motives!

We read in I John 4:19, "We love because He first loved us." I believe that these are some of the most significant words which have ever been written. God's love was the first cause in the universe, and He displayed this to us in the past with the sending of His Son to die for all of humanity. Ultimately, it is He who has created the universe and everything in it including humans. Out of His being flows love, and He allows us to experience this quality as well, though certainly not in the same capacity as His ability to love. Our highest motive must be that of love. Though we will never love as God does, we should never give up on purifying our motives.

On the other hand, there is nothing wrong with making ourselves the best he/she can be. The Apostle Paul wrote to the church in Corinth these words which are contained in 2 Corinthians 5:20, "We are therefore Christ's ambassadors." All of us know the importance of an ambassador. Appointed by the President of the United States, he goes to another country to represent the government and people of the United States. The person who is appointed to this high position must possess outstanding qualities such as intelligence, honesty, competence, and persuasiveness, and of course a certain amount of charm never hurts. Whatever skills we possess, we should sharpen these in order to be an even greater blessing to others. In this life we will be judged and criticized, but much of this has to do with the fact that the person doing the judging is not living life on the highest motivational level. Ask God to do his work in your heart as you re-evaluate your motives and reach for the highest motivation of doing all for the glory of God and the betterment of others.

Developing Patience:

There are very few patient people since most of us are anxious to have projects completed yesterday. In the New Testament, there is an interesting word for patience, which is *hupomeno*. This Greek words means, "to bear, stand firm, hold out, put up with, and remain." The first segment of the word, *hypo*, actually means, "under," so the idea is that of remaining under. We have all heard the expression "under the gun," or "under the pile." Usually that person is stating that there is a task to be done, and it is difficult and laborious, but it will get done. Patience usually takes time as there are very few people who are born that way. Have you every noticed a baby? That little one wants something and wants it now! Waiting is not an option; he is hungry or frustrated, and waiting is not in his vocabulary or makeup at this point.

Patience must develop for most of us. Animals seem to have this ability more than humans. Watch a bird build her nest. She flys away and comes back time and time again with only a mere sprig or twig, but she knows that it can be used. This process goes on for what seems endless, and then you look again, perhaps a few days later, and you see a beautiful nest. Teachers know the importance of patience. In teaching a concept, the instructor may find that the first way it is presented, some of the students may grasp the concept like a steel trap, but more than likely many of them will not. There are always those who just simply have that blank, puzzled look. The teacher exercising great creativity continues to teach, using alternate methods until each student seems to grasp the problem or subject.

Impatience is an expression of selfishness and the belief that somehow the universe revolves around that person. When our twin girls were babies and we would periodically go on trips, it seemed as if our travels had just begun when one of them would impatiently in a somewhat whining voice ask, "Are we there yet?" or "How much longer?"

Some people actually live their whole lives with that attitude. They never mature beyond the ability to see their own problems and issues. You can usually spot these people in lines at the airport or while traveling in congested traffic on the interstate or in a city. They come in all ethnic groups, ages, and social classes.

The Bible has much to say about patience. Certainly most have heard the expression, "the patience of Job." Remember him? The book of Job is one of those Old Testament books with which many are familiar. Job in the first chapter loses everything except his life. His so-called, three friends misread his motives and say that he is suffering because he has sinned. Even his wife is unsupportive and tells him to "Curse God and die!" (Job 1:9) Can you imagine how difficult those days were for Job? By the end of the book, he is doubly blessed. He had to endure a lot to finally receive that blessing, but he was patient. The New Testament speaks of patience too. We read in James 5:7-8: "Be patient, then, brothers, until the Lord's coming. See how the farmer waits for the land to yield its valuable crop and how patient he is for the autumn and spring rains. You too, be patient and stand firm, because the Lord's coming is near."

I once read something about a frog, which can apply to any person who is in a difficult situation. It may have an author, but none was given when presented to me. It is the following:

Two frogs fell into a can of cream,

Or so I've heard it told.

The sides of the can were shiny and steep,

    the cream was deep and cold.

"On, what's the use!" croaked number one.

    "Tis fate, no help's around.

Goodbye, my friend! Goodbye, sad world!"

    And weeping still he drowned.

But number two of sterner stuff,

    Dog-paddled in surprise.

The while he wiped his creamy face,

    and dried his creamy eyes.

"I'll swim awhile at least," he said,

    or so I've heard he said.

"It really wouldn't help the world,

    if one more frog were dead."

An hour or two he kicked and swam,

    not once he stopped to mutter,

but kicked and kicked and swam and kicked,

    Then hopped out, via butter!

While some may find this poem silly, it does describe a deep truth. Everyone wants solutions, but only a few are willing to put forth the extra effort and patiently continue until there is a successful result.

74

Thanking:

Continuous thankfulnesss must be part of our prayers. Have you ever been around a person who complained about everything? More than likely that person was not very popular. We all know about the half full or half empty type person, or the one who wakes up in the morning and says, "Good Lord, it is morning!" instead of "Good morning, Lord." If you want to do an experiment, I am sure that it would be interesting. The first day, think negative thoughts all throughout the day. Don't greet anyone. If you do speak, just complain as much as possible. The next day, think only positive thoughts. Greet as many people as possible, and every time you speak, do so in an uplifting and friendly manner. Compare how you feel at the conclusion of each day. You might even want to keep a journal to help you remember exactly how each day went.

Our moments and days just go better when we are thankful. We love to express our thanks when we are truly grateful. Our food seems to taste better after the giving of thanks, and relationships are fueled and smoothed by the thankfulness of each. Have you ever had this experience? You did something which you believed was significant in value and time for another person. It was not that your motivation was for the person to lavish his or her praise upon you for your time and effort, but after the completion the person offered no words of gratitude or thanks, perhaps just a parting "Goodbye." You maybe experienced several emotions such as hurt, disappointment, and just a sense of being let down by another person. People need to be genuinely thanked and appreciated; there is something reaffirming about this. Many times in the Bible God is presented as having emotions which are somewhat like human beings. We read for example that God loves, becomes angry, is jealous for our affections, displays compassion, desires holiness, and is forgiving. He also loves for His people to thank, praise and worship Him.

The Apostle Paul wrote in I Thessalonians 5:18, "Give thanks in all circumstances." This advice was not coming from a prima donna who had never experienced hardship. Read about his life sometime; it is found in the New Testament. Paul experienced a litany of genuine hardships. He was beaten severely, thrown in jail, shipwrecked, run out of several towns, deprived of food for lengthy periods, and treated many times most shabbily. But yet, he was able to write such words, and he truly meant them. He did not have all the conveniences which we have today, not even the internet! The Roman world was tough; life was cheap and life expectancy was not too long. Paul was able to see beyond his immediate problem to the ultimate solution. What an example!

Trusting:

We live in a world in which genuine trust of another person is rare. You can see the quality of trust in loving families and in some friendships, but trust seems to be like a very precious species which is gradually becoming extinct. We still use some expressions such as, "He is as good as his word," the implication being that this is a person who can be trusted. In biblical times, instead of signing a document and having witnesses, so as to make a promise legal, it was understood that the spoken word and the promise was all that was needed. Do you believe things have changed especially in recent years? Years ago, I was sitting in a used car lot dealer's office, and on his desk was a plaque which read, "Trust Me." Somehow, those words had the opposite effect on me. Whether or nor he was, he certainly knew the importance of trust.

Jesus told his disciples as recorded in John 14:1, "Do not let your hearts be troubled. Trust in God; trust also in me." Jesus' disciples today can have that same confidence and promise. Let's face it. There is a lot in the world today which mitigates against trust, all the way from institutions, to government, professionals, and people who are unknown to us. Some people are not trusting by nature. They were born with certain predispositions or they were taught by parents and people in authority over them to be skeptical and untrusting of almost everything and everyone.

A person who lacks trust seems to be invariably a fearful person. There is much to be fearful about today. The war on terrorism reminds us that we live in a fallen world. The new deadly viruses seem to be mutating at an unprecedented rate of speed. Famine in many African countries is taking countless lives, and Israel and Palestine continue their murdering of one another. If you turn on the news, more than likely you will hear only negative information. This is what makes news move in our culture. Wouldn't it be incredibly refreshing to listen to news which only gave a positive report and dwelled on uplifting issues. Someone might say that sounds so unrealistic; this is not reality. I agree, but it is a matter of emphasis and sorting out what is helpful from that which is not.

America in a sense was built upon the concept of trust. The foundational philosophy was theistic, or a belief and trust in a personal God. Look again at that quarter in your pocket; you will see, "In God we trust" still engraved upon each one.

Those who founded this country knew something about the ultimate source and object of trust. Secure in a relationship with God, one can look at others and reach out to them in a relationship which is marked by trust.

Giving:

Jesus stated as recorded in Acts 20:35, "It is more blessed to give than to receive." I have met numerous people who somehow think if you can reverse that saying to "It is more blessed to receive than to give," then you indeed will be more blessed and happy. God's essential nature is that of giving. After all, He gave to you life, and He wants you to remain

78

in His complete and total will for your life. We read such wonderful passages as Ezekiel 36:26, "I will give you a new heart and put a new spirit within you; I will remove from you your heart of stone and give you a heart of flesh." Without attempting to give all the theological interpretations of this passage, we can say God delights in giving. Again Jesus states in Luke 6:38, "Give, and it will be given to you. A good measure, pressed down, shaken together and running over, will be poured into your lap. For with the measure you use, it will be measured to you." I would be the last person to say that we should give in order that we may get something in return. I would question that kind of motivation. On the other hand, God has set a law, which essentially states if we want more of something in our lives, we must do our part. Passivity is never an option for us.

These are various areas of our lives in which we should be concerned about giving. First, the giving of our time is significant. Time is valuable; we cannot repeat another second and certainly not another day. It is gone, never to be repeated. While we should value our time and use every minute for something significant (which should include some relaxation and rest), we must invest our time in people. It has been said that there are only two things which will last eternally: the Word of God and the souls of people. If we grasp this truth, we will want to be involved in the eternal and not the temporal or that which is transitory. It takes time to help an elderly person, to care for a parentless child, to feed a homeless person and help him turn his life around. Most executives are cleaver about guarding their time and keeping people at a distance unless invited. When a seminary student, a professor told us that many times interruptions are God's appointments. It could be that these interruptions are God's way of gaining our attention, and we should be sensitive to each opportunity that we have to help another person, even if our schedule is disrupted.

We should also give of our talents. Everyone has at least one area of giftedness. I have met a few very rare persons who are multi-gifted. The Bible speaks of spiritual gifts, and we should be aware of these and what God has entrusted to us. However, there are also gifts which a person has naturally. One might be good with finances and possess a wealth of knowledge about the stock market and investing. Another may be good with one's hands and can build almost anything which he/she decides.

Yet another may have the gift of counsel and can bring wisdom and encouragement into the life of one who is depressed or destitute. All of our gifts can complement one another rather than be a source of envy. Rather than being covetous of the skills of another person, thank God for what He has given to you and use this gift to uplift another person.

Compared to most countries in the world, Americans are blessed with possessions. Some have even allowed their possessions to possess them. The Bible presents the principle of giving what we have. In Luke 21:1-4, there was a poor widow and all she had to give were two small copper coins, which was a very small amount of money. Jesus was watching the people give their money, and some of them were very wealthy and were able to give sizable sums of money. Jesus said, "I tell you the truth, this poor widow has put in more than all the others. All these people gave their gifts out of their wealth; but she out of her poverty put in all she had to live on." Again, we see that the motivation for giving is more important than the amount. For the wealthy it was not a sacrifice, but for this woman who gave such a small amount, she truly did give sacrificially, and God was pleased with her.

Think of that person everyone enjoys being around. More than likely he or she is a giving-type person. They may not have much to give financially, but they give of themselves. They are quick with a genuine smile, a helping hand, a kind attitude; they have this aura around them that exudes withconcern for others.

Abandoning Grudges and Anger:

Do you know people who continually hold grudges against others who have wronged them? Perhaps they believe that by being unforgiving, they are actually getting even with the person who has wronged them. I know a person who was slighted by another over thirty years ago, and he still talks about the incident, obviously unable to forgive. I believe that a medical doctor would advise that person to release the animosity, since he is certainly doing himself more harm than the other person. Medical science has proven that unresolved animosities can lead to such maladies as high blood pressure, ulcers, and a host of other physical ailments. If for no other reason, a person should forgive for his own physical and mental well being. Jesus stated in Luke 6:27, "Love your enemies, do good to those who hate you."

Have you ever met a person who seems to be always angry, somewhat like a tornado waiting to happen? It really is not a pleasant experience to see or to be the recipient of such anger. However, there is an appropriate time to be angry. Even Jesus became angry when he drove the money changers out of the temple, yet he did not sin in the process. I believe that there are times when we should be angry. The abuse of a child or an elderly person should cause us to be angry and attempt to intervene in the situation. In Ephesians 4:26, Paul wrote almost two thousand years ago, "Do not let the sun go down while you are still angry." Anger is powerful; it can be both destructive and constructive. We should keep our emotions under control, rather than allowing them to control us. Inappropriate anger is a sin because it can lead to devastation such as fighting and even murder. If we would remember how much we have been forgiven, the temptation to anger will be greatly minimized.

Two years ago, I had the privilege to go to Germany to teach. At the school where I was lecturing was a Christian German professor whom I had known in America twenty years previously. He shared with me something I never knew about him that is a wonderful example of forgiveness and giving up of grudges. In a sense, one could see where it would have been possible for him to continue to harbor a sense of vengeance. His father had become a Nazi and fought against the Allies. He was killed by an American near the end of the war. My friend was only a young child when this happened, and he deeply missed growing up without his father. My father had fought with the Allies during World War II. Though he was not involved in the battle which took the life of my friend's father, he could have harbored some animosity toward me because of association. I sensed none of that. I thought to myself, what an example of giving up grudges. Humanly, anyone would say that he had a right to do so, but there was not even a hint of a grudge.

Desiring the best for others:

We live in a highly competitive environment, especially in America. We love winners and believe that everyone should strive for excellence; the blue ribbon mentality permeates our culture. Second means second best. We naturally do not like the person who brags; he or she grates on us. Jesus gave wonderful words of advice, which we today call the Golden Rule. In Matthew 7:12, Jesus stated; "So in everything, do to others what you would have them do to you." Jesus says we should treat others in a considerate and kind manner. I have discovered that when I take this a step further, that is, I truly want the other person to be fulfilled and have a sense of accomplishment, I have a sense of making that person's load and life easier for him. If that person is happier, there is a chance others will be influenced and there is a domino-like situation occurring. Instead of being surrounded by unhappy, sullen, angry, bitter and vindictive people, you can be in the midst of happy, vibrant, joyful and giving persons.

I have taught thousands of students in both undergraduate and graduate school. I can think of several who were struggling when I first had the opportunity of working with them. What a joy it was to see them progress and blossom into better students. I wanted the best for them; they sensed that and attempted to please me. Some grew at faster rates than others; each was expected to simply do his/her best, and in the dynamic of teaching, responding and learning, growth took place on the part of the teacher and the student. The people of whom you will have the fondest memories are those who cherished you as a person and conveyed that they wanted the best to occur in your life.

∿· CHAPTER FOUR ·∿

SAVING FAITH:
ULTIMATE ASSURANCE

There are many themes in the Bible, but from Genesis to Revelation, the most significant theme is that of salvation or deliverance. Most people today are concerned about the exterior or that which will not last. Many are overly concerned about such possessions as houses, portfolios, cars, and even, or dare I say in some cases, especially their bodies. Certainly plastic surgeons have more than enough work today. On one level people realize that they cannot take their possessions with them, but to look at the life styles of some, one wonders. As someone has humorously said, "I have never seen a U-haul trailer in a funeral procession." With all of our sophistication in especially the physical and biological sciences, we have not progressed to such a state where death is eliminated. Of course, there have been and continue to be some noble efforts. One of the more interesting attempts is that of cryonics. This is where the body is frozen with the anticipation that a cure will be found for whatever took the life of the person, and he or she will be revived.

It is amazing what unusual beliefs one can have if the Bible is not consulted. The Bible says that everyone has a soul or a spirit, and at the moment of physical death, this soul/spirit goes out of the body and is either in God's presence or separated from Him. There is nothing said about this entity entering again into the body as it is now. What the Bible does say is that there will be a resurrected body, which will be similar to the body before death, but of a different substance. The spirit and soul will enter into this resurrected body and for those who have decided by faith to receive Jesus Christ as their personal Saviour will live eternally in this state.

True Christianity is different from every other world religion. I taught world religions for many years at the University of North Carolina, and in my classes, which were always full, a large percentage were agnostic or of another religion. I remember one young lady from Boston who had never seen a Bible; in fact she was not certain what one was. She was twenty-one years old and had lived her entire life in America! Over the

86

years, I have conversed with those who practiced Shinto, Islam, Hinduism, Judaism and Buddhism. I enjoy studying and learning more about world religions; I think every person should familiarize himself with other beliefs. Personally, I was interested in finding an answer to why literally billions followed other world religions besides Christianity.

I discovered that every religion, except for Christianity, asks the participant to do something themselves in order to merit salvation of the soul. For example, Judaism requires that one keep the Ten Commandments, and upon failure, encourages the adherent to once again attempt to keep these mandates. Islam demands that its followers keep the Five Pillars, whereas Buddhism promises release from the cycle of reincarnation in order that one through a process of meditation can reach Nirvana, a state which the Buddha called "perfect mindfulness" or bliss. It is believed in Buddhism that one can be reincarnated innumerable times and in any form of an animal or even an insect!

I have met many who have said something like this. "I cannot accept Christianity because look at what this belief has done in the name of religion. The Crusades were a religious cause. Millions have been slaughtered in the name of religion." I usually reply, "I could not agree with you more!" Religion can be dangerous. What these people are speaking about and describing is not true Christianity, but a counterfeit religion, or even the reference to Christianity to justify their own causes. The word *religion* means "to tie back, or to connect." Religion comes from Latin *re* which means "again" and *ligio* which denotes connection. The word is actually only found a few times in the Bible. In the Greek New Testament, the word is *threskia* and means "religion" or "worship."

In America, try asking the person on the street, "Are you religious?" You will usually get the answer, "Of course, I am an American," or "I attend church." Many will reply that they are a Christian, but have not attended church in decades, do not pray and have not had a thought about God and their souls for a long, long time. These people are not experiencing true Christianity but only its outward shell, if I can describe it that way. True Christianity is a relationship; religion, a word which always invariably leaves me cold, is only the outward form. For example, you have a close friend, one with whom you have been best of friends for thirty years. You have done many activities together, had endless conversations, encouraged each other over the years, and are just comfortable with one another. You know each other's fears, ambitions, abilities, families and essentially know one another as well as is humanly possible. You are best friends and cannot imagine there being another person who could take the place of him or her. You introduce your best friend to an acquaintance, who only hears the name, perhaps shakes hands, and asks some questions which to you may sound superficial. How could your acquaintance even begin to understand your best friend, the one with whom you have shared so much over the past three decades? Your acquaintance may be able to describe, analyze, and even come to some quick conclusions, but on the whole there will be no depth to those descriptions and conclusions.

This is what many do with Christianity. They are able to make some conclusions based on the history and current appearance of the religion, its outward shell, but they have not entered into a relationship with true Christianity. I say true Christianity because much of what calls itself Christian is not. Many of our churches do not tell people how to be right with God, or how to prepare for the life after death. Only in the Bible can one find the ultimate answers to life. I have studied the sacred texts of the other world religions with an open mind, and after having done such for many years, I have concluded that only the Old and New Testaments are the genuine Word of God. I know that this is not political correctness, but if any person would compare the Bible with other religious texts, the differences become obvious almost immediately.

Many people believe that ministers and people who take seriously religion are not the brightest bulbs in the house. Most are not aware of the intellectual heritage of Christianity in America. Do a study of education in America, and you will discover that the reason our Ivy League schools were started in the early eighteenth-century, was for the training of ministers. Instead of sending candidates for ministry back to England to such schools as Oxford and Cambridge, schools such as Harvard, Princeton and Yale were built with a curriculum geared primarily for the study of ministry. At least three languages were required for one to be considered proficient in ministry—Greek, Hebrew, and Latin. Knowledge of these languages was not superficial, but they had to have a working ability with them. Of course, many other disciplines were studied and required for candidacy as a minister or religious leader.

However, true Christianity has been very aware that it is not just a matter about the head—the emotions or the heart is just as important as the intellect. The spiritual life must be nourished throughout one's relationship with God on earth.

Any relationship can become stale and even bitter if not maintained in a loving manner. This is the situation for friends, children and parents as well as married couples. The relationship must grow, there must be communication, respect for one another, and a genuine delighting in the other's presence. Certainly, it is no different with one's relationship with God. Though He is all-powerful, He has emotions which we too possess. There must be daily communication with Him, reading of and meditating upon portions of the Bible, at least weekly church attendance and sharing with others as much as possible one's faith journey. These are essential ingredients for a strong, healthy, and growing Christian life.

The name Christian has been abused and misunderstood for many centuries, and as previously stated, some use the term in reference to themselves when perhaps they have not experienced the reality of what a true Christian is. For example, I have met many people who are very proud of their heritage. If someone would ask them, "Where are you from or what is your genealogy?" they would reply that they are Welsh, German, Russian or Swedish. More than likely they have never been to such countries, they may not even know one name of their ancestors. They have no personal awareness of what the terrain of their ancestral lands look like, yet they proudly state their connection to such a place. I have met many who have said they are Christians, yet they know nothing about Christianity—what they understand is something like a strange land to them. They have never truly experienced it. So much which is called Christian fits into a similar pattern—it is a label without substance, used by many who do not understand or truly know its dynamic, power and reality. They have read about Christianity, perhaps even know some of its history before the Protestant Reformation and after.

Before the Reformation, in essence there was only one major branch in Christianity—Catholicism, both Roman and the Eastern Orthodox Church which was predominant in Russia and Greece especially. The Protestant Reformation began in 1517, when Martin Luther posted his Ninty-Five Theses on the church door in a little east German town of Wittenberg. From this protest, the movement spread throughout Europe and eventually to America. All of our many denominations in Protestantism go back in a sense to the protesting of the thirty-four year old monk, Martin Luther. There are about 2,000 denominations in America such as various Baptist, Methodist and Presbyterian groups, whereas in Europe there is still primarily the state church for Protestantism.

Why are there so many denominations in America? Why cannot there just be one or maybe two? Think of it as a family scattering. I grew up in a family of four boys and one girl. We all are distinct from one another with our own gifts, likes and dislikes. I am not sure it would have been the best for all of us to stay in the same house all our lives with one another, never marry, develop in our career, and seek outside interests. When each was mature, he or she began his own family and lived separately from the others, though still close emotionally. Though this example is not perfect, think of all the denominations as members of the same family, but because of sociological factors, emphases on various doctrines, ethnic considerations, and preferences in worship, there have are many denominations. On the other hand, there are some denominations which do not emphasize what other Christian religious groups would consider to be important, or even essential to believe in order to be right with God.

Every religion has two bottom lines: how to live well in this life and how to find complete joy in the life after death. As previously stated, all the world religions, and even the various belief systems outside of Christianity such as Mormonism, Jehovah's Witness, Christian Science, Unity and Unitarianism, all teach in order to reach this perfect state you must perform. True Christianity, that is, the kind of Christianity which teaches what is found in the Bible, says you can do nothing. You yourself cannot perform enough, or do enough works to please God. Why? Because true Christianity teaches that salvation by works is impossible. Think of the holiest person you know and then the evilest one you know. In God's sight, on one level they are the same. Both are humans, and both are not able to achieve perfection through their own ability. The Bible and true Christianity state that a person must be perfect! When one first hears this, it causes some confusion. How can a person be perfect? We can't! The only way possible is through the perfection of another. Jesus Christ is the God-man; He is eternal but in a point in time He took on flesh and became a human being. This is what Christmas celebrates—God becoming man. He lived a perfect life though in his human nature he was tempted. Yet he never sinned; those many temptations were real. He became hungry, weary, and even angry, but never once did he cross the line to actually commit a sin. He was perfect, and because of this he has the credential, the only one who does, to be the Saviour for all of humanity.

The Bible states in Romans 3:23, "All have sinned and fallen short of the glory of God." In Romans 6:23, we read, "For the wages of sin is death, but the free gift of God is eternal life in Christ Jesus our Lord." Romans 8:1 promises, "There is therefore now no condemnation for those who are in Christ Jesus." It is possible to have the very own righteousness of Jesus Christ according to the Bible. The Apostle Paul writes in 2 Corinthians 5:21, "He made Him who knew no sin to be sin on our behalf, that we might become the righteousness of God in Him." True Christianity believes that the Bible is literally God's Word, or His promise to every human being who will come to Him His way. A person can be seen in God's sight as righteous as His own Son, Jesus Christ. But the question is, what is God's way and how does one come to Him?

Westerners, in particular Americans, love to do things their own way. We like the lyrics in Frank Sinatra's song, "I did it my way," which seems to capture the ethos of a great many Americans today. We want to achieve, and yes, we want to do it our way. This causes problems especially for the person who first hears what the Gospel is. The word Gospel is a Greek New Testament word and means "good news" or the good news about salvation in Christ and the hope of living for Him in this life and the life to come.

One of the clearest passages in the Bible concerning eternal life and what God's requirements are is found in John the third chapter. A wealthy and powerful man, who was actually a theologian of sorts, did not fully understand what he had been teaching for years came to see Jesus. His name was Nicodemus. The Bible says it was at night; apparently he was did not want to be seen. Jesus told him that he needed to be "born again." Of course Nicodemus did not understand this; he actually thought that Jesus was telling him he needed to come out of his mother's womb a second time! Then Jesus gives what many consider the clearest passage in all the Bible concerning how a person can be right in God's eyes; Jesus said as recorded in John 3:16, "For God so loved the world, that he gave His one and only Son, that whoever believes in Him should not perish, but have eternal life." Martin Luther called this one verse, "the Gospel in a nutshell." Some of the world's greatest philosophers and theologians such as Karl Barth admitted that they did not fully understand the magnitude of this verse. Yet a mere child understands enough to believe this verse and to receive Jesus by faith, true faith, and pass from a life of darkness into light.

The Bible states about 200 times that the condition for experiencing

God's grace or eternal life is by faith only. Some groups want to emphasize the importance of baptism, but most would say that while it is very
important to be baptized, if one has received Jesus Christ by faith and
has not had the opportunity of baptism, he or she is a child of God and
will experience the joys of eternal life with Him and others who have
made that decision.

A passage which I have always found clear and meaningful is
Ephesians 2: 8-9, which states,

> For by grace you have been saved through faith; and that not of yourselves, it
> is the gift of God; not as a result of works, that no one should boast. For we
> are His workmanship, created in Christ Jesus for good works, which God pre-
> pared beforehand, that we should walk in them. (NIV, Zondervan, 1985)

Faith in the Bible is much more than knowing something or only head
knowledge. Theologians explain biblical faith as involving three compo-
nents: intellect, emotions, and will, or in more basic terms knowing,
experiencing, and choosing or believing in something or someone.
Maybe this illustration is helpful. The story is told about a man walking
the tight rope across Niagara Falls. He went across, and the large crowd
cheered. Next he pushed a wheel barrel across, and again the crowd
cheered wildly. He then asked, "How many think that I will be able to
carry a person across in the wheel barrow?" Again, the crowd cheered
encouragingly and shouted, "Yes!" He then asked, "Who will volunteer
for such a venture?" No one answered, and you could see the doubt and

fear in the faces of many. This is obviously an example of what faith is not. When a child climbs a small tree and the father asks him or her to jump into his arms, and the child does, this is an example of faith. The child knows he will have to trust his father, and he has complete confidence in him. Ultimately it is God who knows who has put saving faith in His Son, and when that truly happens a miracle occurs; a man, woman or child is saved, born again, removed from the great majority who will not make that decision.

Many ask about the importance of works. Why are works not able to save? There is a logical answer. The Bible says that if we commit one sin, that is enough to disqualify us from God's heaven. Everyone has sinned at least one time; in fact, the Bible says in James 2:10 that even if we fail to keep one point of the Law, we are guilty in breaking all of the Law in God's eyes. There is only one person who has ever lived perfectly, Jesus Christ, and He has the credentials to save anyone who will acknowledge and receive Him or trust in Him by faith alone. Works are of vital importance, but not to gain salvation. One must have a life characterized by doing good works after experiencing God's gift of salvation. James 2:17 states: "Even so faith, if it has no works, is dead, being by itself." A person who claims to have been saved by faith, but is lacking in goodness or Christian virtues, should seriously question if the conversion is genuine. On the other hand, every true Christian after salvation continues to grow and to be more and more like Jesus, though ultimate perfection in this life will never be possible.

✥ CONCLUSION ✥

No one is guaranteed another day, and the Bible is clear that after death, there will not be another chance. I remember as a child seeing my great grandfather on his death bed. At the time he made a decision for Christ, he was eighty-eight years old. Though he lived a good life and was a good man, how much more meaningful his life could have been if he had decided even as a child to receive Christ as Savior. An early decision for Christ would have meant over half a century of serving Christ instead of the world. He was most fortunate that he did not die before deciding. I have met many who have said that they have all the time in the world, when the fact is no one knows how much time he or she has. So many think they have to have "fun" first and then become serious about their spiritual lives. They do not realize that the most exciting and fulfilling life is living for God and allowing Him to live through their lives. Statistics show that after the late teen years, only a small percentage will come to Christ. The heart grows more and more callous toward spiritual matters the older a person becomes. Make the decision today! If you have already done so, tell another person and continue to live joyfully and victoriously. One thing for sure, you will have a heavenly future!

KINGDOM BOUND: OUR JOURNEY OF JOY

100

www.ingramcontent.com/pod-product-compliance
Lightning Source LLC
Chambersburg PA
CBHW060346100426
42812CB00003B/1153